An Account of the Courts of Prussia and Hanover;

Sent to a Minister of State in Holland

John Toland (1670-1722)

TMP

Publications

Original author, John Toland (1670-1722). First published in 1705. This edition has been faithfully reproduced from the original and re-published in a modern typeface, with original spelling, emphasis and formats preserved.

This edition is published by The Manuscript Publisher, 2013

General Editor: J.N. Duggan

ISBN: 978-0-9576729-1-8

A CIP Catalogue record for this book is available from the British Library

Digitisation, typesetting, cover design by DocumentsandManuscripts.com

Cover image illustrations have been sourced and used courtesy of Wikimedia Commons. They include: *Theater of the World, or a New Atlas of Maps and Representations of All Regions, Edited by Willem and Joan Blaeu*, 1645; *Hannover von Osten aus gesehen*, Von Matthäus Merian 1654 geschaffen; Coat of arms of Royal Prussia after 1450; Crest from the flag of the Kingdom of Hanover.

Publishing solutions for the digital age. For more information please visit: www.TheManuscriptPublisher.com

The only known image of John Toland (1670-1722)

Contents

Foreword

In 1701, John Toland was a member of Lord Macclesfield's delegation, which travelled to Hanover to deliver the Act of Settlement to Sophia, the Dowager-Electress. This Act named her and her Protestant, legitimate, descendants as 'Heirs of Great Britain' should Queen Anne die without issue, so the delegation was made very welcome! Whilst there, he became a favourite of Sophia and her daughter Sophia Charlotte, the Queen in Prussia and spent some time both in Hanover and Berlin.

He wrote this description of the Courts of Prussia and Hanover to an unnamed Dutch Minister of State, sometime between 1701 and 1705. The original was written in French - the language of diplomacy - and, in 1705, he translated it into English, at the request of the sixth Duke of Somerset, whom Toland addresses in the Dedication. The Duke had been appointed, in 1702, to the post of Master of the Horse to Queen Anne.

Despite his denials, he lays the flattery on thick when describing members of the ruling families. Sophia of Hanover and her daughter Sophia Charlotte were indeed remarkable and intelligent women and George I was, in fact, a far more able and astute man than he is generally credited with being. Frederick William, the Crown Prince of Prussia, however, was a violent bully (his visits to Hanover were dreaded by his far gentler cousin, George August) but, since he was the apple of both his mother's and his grandmother's eyes, Toland would never have dared to say this. Likewise, Frederick I's notorious expenditure on precious stones was outlandish and ill-advised, but Toland contents himself with repeating the criticisms of others without endorsing them. The only flaw that he will admit to in any of the royal personages, is that Sophia Charlotte was somewhat too plump - which was true, but unkind! He was, actually, one of her greatest admirers: she was the 'Serena' to whom he dedicated his book, *Letters to Serena.*

After 300 years, his account is still very readable and gives us an accessible and engaging picture of life in those German courts, and of the people who inhabited them at the turn of the 17th to 18th Century.

Members of the Courts of Prussia and Hanover in 1705

William of Orange, deceased: 1650-1702, King of England, Scotland, Ireland and Wales (here referred as The Late King).

Charles Seymour, 6th Duke of Somerset: 1662-1748, Master of the Horse to Queen Anne. Known as 'The Proud Duke'.

Prussia:

William Frederick, The Elector of Brandenburg, deceased: 1620-1688; The Great Elector, (here referred to as The Late Elector). Married:

(1) **Luise Henriette**, deceased: 1627-1677; daughter of Prince Henry of Orange-Nassau.

(2) **Sophia Dorothea**, deceased: 1636-1689; daughter of Duke of Holstein-Sonderburg-Glucksburg.

Frederick I: 1657-1713, King in Prussia 1701-1713; son of The Great Elector and Luise of Orange-Nassau.

Sophie Charlotte deceased: 1668-1705; Queen in Prussia 1701-1705; daughter of Ernst August, Elector of Hanover and Sophia of Hanover.

Frederick William: 1688-1749; The Prince Royal; son of Frederick I and Sophie Charlotte, later King Frederick William I, King in Prussia.

Philip William of Brandenburg-Schwedt: 1669-1711; son of The Great Elector and Sophia Dorothea of Holstein-Sonderburg-Glucksburg.

Johanna Charlotte of Anhalt-Dessau: 1682-1750; wife of Philip of Brandenburg-Schwedt.

Hanover:

Ernst August, Elector of Hanover deceased: 1629-1698.

Sophia, Dowager-Electress of Hanover: 1630-1714; daughter of Frederick V of the Palatinate and Elizabeth Stuart, King and Queen of Bohemia; widow of Ernst August.

George William, Duke of Zell: 1624-1705; brother of Ernst August and father-in-law of George Lewis.

George Lewis, Elector of Hanover: 1660-1727; son of Ernst August and Sophia and future George I of England.

George August: 1683-1760; son of George Lewis and Sophie Dorothée of Celle; later George II of England.

Sophia Dorothea: 1687-1757; daughter of George Lewis and Sophie Dorothée of Celle; later Queen in Prussia.

Maximilian William: 1666-1726; son of Ernst August and Sophia.

Ernst August junior: 1674-1726; youngest son of Ernst August and Sophia; later Bishop of Osnabruck.

Melusine von Schulenburg: 1667-1743; lady-in-waiting to Sophia and mistress to George Lewis; later Duchess of Kendal and Munster.

Sophia von Kielmansegg: 1675-1717; illegitimate daughter of Ernst August and Countess Clara von Platen; later Countess of Leinster and Darlington.

Clara von Platen deceased: 1648-1700; Mistress of Ernst August and wife of Count von Platen.

Gottfried William von Liebniz: 1646-1716; the famous philosopher, librarian to the Court of Hanover.

Gerhardt Walter Molanus: 1633-1722; Lutheran Abbot of Loccum and a frequent visitor to the Court of Hanover.

Fitton Charles Gerard deceased: 1665-1701; 3rd Earl of Macclesfield, Whig politician.

Giovanni Battista Bononcini: 1670-1747; Italian composer and cellist, spent some time at the Court of Berlin

AN

ACCOUNT

OF THE

COURTS

OF

Pruſſia and Hanover;

Sent to a Miniſter of State
in Holland

BY

Mr. TOLAND.

LONDON,

Printed by JOHN DARBY in Bartholo-
mew Cloſe. M.DCC.V.

Facsimile of the original edition, published in 1705.
Source: The Open Library.

The Dedication

To the most Noble, Highborn, and Mighty Prince,
CHARLES
Duke of Somerset, Marquiss and Earl of Hertford, Viscount Beauchamp of Hatche, Baron Seymour of Trowbridg, Master of the Horse to the Queen's Majesty, and one of her most honorable Privy-Council, Chancellor of the University of Cambridg, and Knight of the most noble Order of the Garter.

May it please your Grace,

THO the Advantages of a noble Birth contribute above all things to a generous Education, to inspire Men with large and elevated Thoughts, and to incite them betimes to worthy and heroic Deeds; and tho your illustrious Family is not only most signally distinguish'd in these Ilands, but likewise over all the Continent of Europe, and much further; tho it be eternally memorable in History for so often and so strenuously defending the Rights of Englishmen, for being so happily instrumental to introduce the Reformation of Religion among us, and in filling our Imperial Throne with the most belov'd and regretted of Princes: Yet these are not the Reasons why I address your Grace with this Account of two Courts you greatly respect, and which was written at the Request of another very eminent Minister.

NOR is it, my Lord, because you have acquitted your self with such universal Applause in the several Posts, which were graced under more than one King with your management, as you still continue to do those wherein you are now intrusted by your Royal Mistriss; which things, tho deserving high Commendation, yet are common to you with som others: as there be many worthy Patriots, who share the Glory with your Grace of having faithfully serv'd the late King WILLIAM while alive, and vindicating his Memory after his Death from the meanest, falsest, and most malicious Aspersions; an evident Demonstration how affectionatly you approve his Cause, as you sincerely lov'd his Person.

NEITHER, lastly, is it for any of your excellent Qualitys, wherby I cou'd particularly recommend to the World my own Penetration and Judgment, for discovering or approving them sooner than others; but I joyfully embrace this lucky Minute to pay an acknowledgment to your Grace, which Thousands want but a fit Opportunity to proclaim, I mean, for that singular ZEAL and COURAGE you have lately shown (above all others) in asserting the most divine Cause of LIBERTY, against those who wou'd persecute Men (obedient to our Constitution) for the sincerity of their Profession in variable Opinions, about matters of bare Speculation or indifferent Practice; against such as wou'd impiously subvert the ordinary Course of our most wise and equal Laws; against all, that in Opposition to the establish'd Succession of the House of Hanover, wou'd disturb the Tranquillity of our own, no less than prevent the stricter Conjunction of the neighboring Nation of Scotland: thus most ungratefully endeavoring to molest the Reign of the best of Queens, who so earnestly desires, and so triumphantly procures *the Good and Happiness of all her People.*

PERMIT me to tell you, my Lord, that no History can instance the Place, where the Nobles were more solidly and effectually popular in a free Government, than they are at this present in England: for who among us is or can be ignorant of their tender Concern for her Majesty's Allys and the Protestant Line? their hearty Zeal against France, and the pretended JAMES the Third? their so firmly maintaining the just Liberty of the Subject, and the lawful Prerogative of the Prince? their solicitous Care in preserving the ordinary Course of Justice, both in the several Countrys, and in the solemn Tribunals of Westminster-Hall? their impartial detecting such Abuses as have insensibly crept into many Branches of the Administration? their prudent defeating the villanous Conspiracys (whether at home or abroad) against her Majesty's person and Government? their incouraging of Trade, promoting of Industry, rewarding Merit, and punishing Offenders?

FOR these most general Benefits (express'd in so many Addresses, Resolutions, Speeches, and Representations, of incomparable Force, Politeness, and Eloquence) they are no less admir'd and reverenc'd, than for their vigorous Efforts to have them put in due Execution. In these and many other particulars, the Eys of all Men are peculiarly fixt on your Grace, as their principal Spring and Mover: the impotent Envy and Detraction of the worst, being amply overbalanc'd by the unbounded Love and Praises of the best.

BUT that I may no longer unwillingly interrupt your noble Designs, so advantageous to our Queen and Country, so seasonable and necessary for the welfare of Europe, and so truly glorious to your own Name and Posterity, I shall only add, that, with the most profound Respect and Gratitude, I am,

My Lord,

Your Grace's most faithful,
most humble, and most
obedient Servant,

J. TOLAND

The PREFACE.

1. WHEN I was last at the Court of Prussia, I sent the following Relations to Holland in a familiar and negligent Stile, as Letters are usually written, and in a different Language from ours. Now that they are thought fit to be made public, I have with the utmost exactness express'd my Originals; not only as to the very Manner, but likewise in reference to the Contents, which in both are perfectly the same: for as in altering or omitting any thing I cou'd not be just to the Truth; so for adding nothing at present (tho never so material) I want not my Reasons, among which I reckon it the least, that hereafter I may gratify the curious with a much larger Account of the same and other Places.

2. CERTAIN Terms (but very few) which are promiscuously us'd in both Languages, as Menagery, Cascades, and the like, I have left as I found 'em; tho in som others, the better to be understood, I dispens'd, with Custom: and thus a jet d'eau (for example) I have literally but coarsly translated a Spout. More Instances of this nature may occur; but this is a matter that, as I have little practis'd it, gives me yet less trouble.

3. THE Person with whom I corresponded knew my Entertainment so well, and how I far'd in every place, that I needed not to speak much of my self, as

Travellers commonly do; and the little I have Said was unavoidably occasion'd by the Nature and Order of the Narrative I have made according to his Instructions, without any View or Permission at that time to print it. But I assure those who may be displeas'd at my receiving any Honor or favors from Persons so highly dignify'd, that tho I have som Reason to think the better of my self for it, yet I think not the worse of any others.

4. MANY who were ne'er abroad, and have form'd very odd Notions to themselves of all other States and Princes, will be ready to accuse me of Flattery; and som others will be apt to believe, that Obligations from Superiors may gain upon a Man somtimes to represent things in a better Light than they deserve, tho without any design of imposing on the Public: but taking wholly on my self all the Reflections I have made, I appeal for matters of Fact to the English who have bin at both Courts since the Act of Succession;[1] *and they are not a few of all Qualitys, Conditions, and Partys. Judgments it's true may differ; and God forbid that in this particular any Man shou'd be abridg'd of his Liberty. Som therfore may probably condemn what I so much approve in the Buildings, Inscriptions, Statues, and Medals of one Prince; while they, who admire all these, may dislike what I yet more approve in the political, religious, and domestic Maxims of another Prince. But I desire not to be misunderstood, since they are only the bare Facts that I recommend to every one's Consideration; and that I think my self but one of many Judges, without expecting any deference to my Opinion.*

5. AS to the Title of Royal Highness *which I give in these Letters to the Princess SOPHIA Electress Dowager of Hanover, the Person to whom I wrote them dos the same, not merely as she's the presumtive Successor of the English Throne, but rather as being, the Daughter of a Prince who was acknowleg'd by the Nations of England and Holland for King of Bohemia. The Ministers of som foren Princes (who own'd her Father for no more than Elector Palatin) use the same Stile, and I have seen the Letters of som Princes themselves directed* to her Royal Highness*: but, few People doing it in England because she's not so nam'd in our Liturgy, I wou'd inform the Reader, that it was not out of Ignorance or Inadvertence I gave her that Title, but from Persuasion and Example.*

6. I HAVE subjoin'd, as a proper Appendix to these Papers, the Oath *for abjuring the pretended* JAMES *the Third, and all other Pretenders whatsoever; and also the* Clause *that makes it High-Treason to write or speak, or to commit any other overt Act, against the Protestant Succession in the House of Hanover. They are Pieces of which no body ought to be ignorant, which way soever their Inclinations may be fixt: and perhaps by this Conveyance, they may fall into the Hands of many that never read them.*

7. FOR the rest, I have bin so scrupulous in giving these Letters as they were first written, that I have left them sign'd with my Surname only, according to a prevailing Custom in those Countrys. The same Reason kept me from making large Additions (as now without suspicion of Flattery I might) to the Queen of Prussia's unequal'd Character, that Sheet being sent me to revise the very Day I receiv'd the most surprising News of her Majesty's Death. And this is all I have to premonish the Reader.

ERRATA.

PAGE 12. Line 3. for *Quarters* read *Wards*.
P. 18. l. 5. for *first* r. *third*.
P. 23. l. 28. for *hinder* r. *further*.
P. 32. l. 13. for *Park and* r. *Park, and*.
P. 35.1. 26. for *Dessau* r. *Anhalt-Dessau*.
P. 51. l. 17. after *Bokkenberg*, add *or Brokkenberg and Blocksberg*.
P. 53. l. 4. after *Lodges* add *or Stalls*.
P. 60. l. 26. for *Englishman* r. *English-Gentleman*.
P. 70. l. 12. *in the Morea* was a mistake for his Brother who was there.

A
RELATION
SENT FROM
Berlin to the *Hague*,
August 18. *N.S.* 1702.

SIR,

1. THE same Light of Reason that forbids us to flatter Vice, dos always oblige us to be just to Virtue: and therfore a Man, who has the Happiness to appertain to a free Country, will never fear the Censure of the envious or the interested, no more than the Displeasure of Princes or their Ministers; provided all that he advances be justify'd by incontestable Facts, that he relates them in a manner becoming the Persons and the Subject of his Discourse; and that the things speak better of themselves, than he was capable to describe them by his Pen. As from such a one, prepare your self, SIR, to hear somtimes certain Reflections or observations that will not please every Body, tho they may not be ungrateful to you, nor in their nature impertinent. I promis'd at my departure to send you som Remarks on the King of Prussia's Country, on his

Government, his Court, and his numerous Houses. This I shall do at present in a general way, begging your Patience, till I be able to enter into a greater detail, when I shall have more insight and less business.

2. BUT first I must satisfy the last Question you were pleas'd to propose to me, why the Inns and Public Houses of Entertainment, on the great Roads in Westphalia, and some other Parts of Germany, are so ill provided with Beds, Provisions, and most things for accommodating Travellers and Strangers? The reason of it is, that the Country is not near so well peopled, nor the Ways so much frequented by Passengers, as in England and Holland. With us, you know, the Citys, Burroughs, and Villages, being so thick sown and so near one another, there is always a great number of Persons passing and repassing, and the very Neighbourhood is an Inticement for many to go from home; besides that Trade is the Cause, that Crouds of People, who have a mutual Dependence on each other, are continually beating the Road. Add to this, that our Stage-Coaches, Waggons, Boats, and other Carriages, are not only very regular in their Turns, but that, counting one time with another, they are generally fill'd with Passengers, The Innkeepers therfore are careful to provide whatever may serve for the Convenience, Pleasure, or Necessity of all Kinds and Ranks of People, being certain of receiving the Mony they have laid out with considerable Profit. And if it shou'd happen somtimes (as it cannot but do) that

there is not Company enough to consume what they dress, yet they are at no loss; for besides what the Family eats of it, and what they can sell to their poorer Neighbors, they get themselves sufficiently reimburs'd by the next Comers, in which Art the Innkeepers of England and Holland are the most experienc'd Masters in the World.

3 NOW, on the contrary, in these Parts of Germany which you have specify'd, the Country not being peopl'd a fifth part, there being little or no Trade, and very few Travellers, there is not a Prospect of Gain enough to make the Innkeepers furnish their Houses with Beds or Utensils, nor to lay up any Store of good Provisions, nor ever to dress a Bit of Meat beforehand: so that a Man is very happy if he meets with clean Straw wheron to sleep, without expecting Sheets or Coverings; and he has no great reason to complain if he gets any thing to eat, tho without the Service of Plates, Forks, or Napkins. He must be content to have the Cows, Swine, and Poultry for his Fellow-Lodgers, and to go in at the same Passage that the Smoak comes out, for there's no other vent for it but the Door; which makes Foreigners commonly say, that the People in Westphalia enter their Houses by the Chimny. This is the reason why their Beef and Hams are so finely prepar'd and ripen'd; for the Fireplace being backwards, the Smoak must spread over all the House before it gets to the Door, which makes every thing within of a russet or sable Color, not excepting the Hands and Faces of the meaner sort. Thus what

we many times attribute to Art, is only the effect of Ignorance or Chance. But as to the badness of their Entertainment I must add, that the People of Condition who travel are very uncertain, having Relays of their own; and that those, who go by the Post-Waggons, are seldom at much Expence. But were there as many People on the Road, or that their Arrival were any thing regular, I make no manner of doubt, but that in proportion they wou'd be as well treated as with us; which really happens in all Parts of Germany, where the Country is more populous or more frequented. But then you must pay a better Price than in those Places which are thinly inhabited; tho I am not to instruct you, SIR, that the dearness of certain things is not always so much a sign of their scarcity, as of the abundance of other things, especially Men and Mony. But whether this mighty want of People, and consequently of all the Fruits of Industry, be owing to the badness of the Country, which yet is not the worst I ever saw, for 'tis a much richer Soil and better water'd than Scotland; or whether it be owing to the arbitrary Administration of the Governors, who (provided they enrich themselves) neither have any Concern for the ease and welfare of their Subjects, nor consequently any true Knowledge of Traffick, Improvement of Land, or Political Oeconomy: which of these, I say, or whether any of them be the Cause, I will not determin, as not being so desir'd by you, and believing I shou'd take upon me to teach my Master.

4. AS for what regards Robbers and Highway-men, how they have bin exterminated out of these Countrys, and by what Regulations they are kept from breaking out again, I shall take another time to give you my Reasons or my Opinion: but now I will delay no longer to communicat to you those Remarks you have so much press'd me to send concerning the Court and Country of his Majesty the King of Prussia. I may truly say, that, without asking Questions of any Body, a Traveller may distinguish this Country by most sensible effects, as soon as he enters it. The Highways are here kept in better Order than elswhere, the Posts are more regular, public Carriages are more expeditious; and wherever the Ways divide themselves, there are strong Pillars erected, with as many pointing Arms as there are Roads, bearing, in Letters cut or painted, the Names of the next Stage, and telling the number of Miles to that Place, as well as from the last out of which you set forth. And this method is exactly observ'd throout all his Majesty's Dominions, which are so large and numerous, extending from his Dutchy of Cleves on your Confines, all the way cross the Empire to the Kingdom of Poland. Having come to Berlin this Year by the way of Hamburgh, as the last Year from Hanover; and having seen not only Halberstadt, Magdenburg, and Brandenburg on the one side, but likewise several smaller Citys, Burroughs and numberless Villages on the one and the other side; I presently took notice, that (besides the Ways) all the Churches as well of the Country as of the Towns were kept in so good a repair as I never

saw the like, being most of 'em newly plaister'd, whiten'd, or adorn'd in som other manner; the Church-yards being inclos'd with durable Walls of Stone or Brick, the Gates being generally large, and many new Steeples rais'd, not inferiour to the old ones: but whether in being lately built from the Ground, or in being repair'd and beautify'd, I cou'd not remark one Church that was defective in any thing. I say this of the Churches both of the Lutherans and the Calvinists, for they have their Church-yards, Steeples, Bells, and such other things alike; and not as with you in Holland, or with us in England, where the tolerated Churches have not those Marks of Honor (as I may call them,) or where the Poverty or Modesty of the Congregations dos not affect them. You may perceive by this instance, how great a regard the King has to the Beauty of public Buildings, no less than for the Conveniences of public Worship. And indeed all the Roads, Statues, Fountains, Edifices, and other Structures belonging to the Public, ought to be every where magnificent, as well as kept in good Order; in both which respects England comes mighty short of Holland. These are not only an Ornament to a Country, and the Indications of a noble Spirit and great Wealth, of Wisdom and Frugality in the Magistrats; but even the meanest of the vulgar are fond of such things, not merely as fine Objects that make delightful Impressions on their Senses, but they consider them likewise as their own Property (which certainly they are) in common with all those who contribute to their founding or preservation: just in the same manner that the Street belongs no less to a Cobler than to a Duke; and they value themselves accordingly.

5. EXCEPTING the Places about the Capital City of Berlin, (which is situated in a very sandy Territory, and too much cover'd with Woods) the Country is at least twice as well peopl'd, and in many Parts a great deal more than Westphalia. I met many more Passengers on the Road, I perceiv'd all Men employ'd about som business or other; and I saw several Trades and Manufactures as I past along; every thing being at once in a perpetual motion, and yet the whole enjoying a most profound repose. You have too accurat a knowledg of Nature, SIR, to admit of any hazard in the Universe, being fully persuaded that every Effect has its natural and necessary Cause: and I make no question but you'l confess with me, that all these things are produc'd by the gentle, wise, and watchful Government of the late Elector, and of the present King, who can never do better than scrupulously to follow the Lessons of so great a Master; and in reality he has surpast them on many accounts, which I shall show to you as the proper Occasions may offer themselves.

6. THERE is no Prince that more successfully practises those Maxims which to the ignorant seem contradictory, but without which nevertheless there cou'd be no Society or Government; and we may say, that God himself preserves the World by the Oppositions of Heat and Cold, of Gravity and Levity, of hard and fluid Bodys, whence proceeds

the admirable Harmony of all things. Thus a Prince ought to be mild himself, while his Laws are severe; he must be impartial towards his Subjects, yet distinguish Merit; and moderat in his Imposts, but lawfully exacting all that is requisit for the good of the State. In a word, you'l never see a great number of People, where there is not a manifest safety for their Persons and Possessions; a Consumtion at Home for the Productions of their Industry or their Lands, and a Market for the same things abroad, which makes them of course to be exported to foren Countrys, and other necessary Goods to be imported thence in exchange, or, what gives us the Ballance of Trade, Mony. Where these things are seen, one may not more infallibly conclude Smoak to be a sign of Fire, than that the Sovereign is religiously observant of the Laws, a Preserver of Liberty, an Incourager of Arts, a Protector of the good, a Punisher of the bad, and that he believes his Revenues more secure in the Purses of his Subjects than in his own Treasury: for those Princes that require too much of their Subjects, will get nothing in a small time; wheras such as limit themselves to what is necessary, will never want an Overplus in case of need. But where to find many of this sort among the Despotic Princes of our Time, is an Inquiry no less difficult, than nice and dangerous.

7. ALL those Effects I have bin relating to you of the Justice, Moderation, and Prudence of King FREDERIC, are literally true, and they appear every where; but no where in greater Lustre, than in his

ordinary Residence of Berlin. This City, which is indifferently spacious, but extremely fine, is divided into two principal Parts, wherof the first, which is the old Town, is again subdivided into three ~~Quarters~~ Wards,[2] namely Berlin, Colen, and the Werder. The new Town, which is likewise begun to be fortify'd, is one part of it call'd Friderickstadt, and the other part Dorothéestadt, from the Names of the late Elector and Electress, so that the whole City consists of five Wards, not to mention the Suburbs. The Streets are very large and noble, much better pav'd than is usual in Germany, and planted in most parts of the Town with Rows of Trees as in your Provinces, which serves for profit as much as for pleasure, tho little practis'd in England. There are fine Canals that cross and separate the several Wards, with Draw-Bridges after the model of those in Holland, and as handsom. The new Houses are mostly built after the best Tast of Architecture, being generally beautify'd on the outside, and not always ill-furnish'd within; the few old Houses that remain, being in respect of the others as ragged and deform'd Dwarfs compar'd with gentile and proper Men.

8. THERE are in this City many things worthy the Curiosity of Strangers. In the Palace is a Library, which has an annual Fund to augment and to maintain it. The Books are well chosen, numerous, and in good case; yet it wants much of being equal to the Library at Wolfembuttle, tho it might receive a noble addition by his Excellency Baron SPANHEIM's Books, which the King has purchased,

and are kept apart in the Chancery. No other account needs to be given of them, when they are known to have bin collected by that incomparable Antiquary, polite Scholar, and approv'd Statesman. Near to the Royal Library is a Cabinet of Raritys, which may be properly call'd a rich Treasure, containing many wonderful effects of Nature and Art, such as are not easily seen in other Courts; to which must be join'd his Majesty's curious Collection of Medals, of both which a particular account may be seen in several Volums, already publish'd, of Monsieur BERGER's *Thesaurus Brandeburgicus*. The Moderns have produc'd nothing that exceeds the Equestrian Statue, which by Order of the King is elevated to the Honor of his illustrious Father (the greatest General of the former Age) on the fine Bridg of square Stone, which his Majesty has caus'd to be built over a Branch of the Spré. The Man and the Horse are one intire piece, which was cast at once; it weighs 3000 Quintals of Metal, and cost forty thousand Crowns. The Pedestrian Statue for his Majesty resembles him very much, and is to be set up in the Area of the Arsenal, which is almost finish'd, in the Quarter call'd the Werder. It is a massy square Building, where Architecture and Expence, where Convenience and Ornament have not bin dealt by a scanty Hand, and wherof a great part is already stor'd with very fair pieces of Artillery and other Arms, which are kept in good order.

9. NEAR to the Arsenal is a Sluce, formerly of Timber, but now wholly of wrought Stone, and

accompany'd with a large wet Dock, which may well be call'd the Port of Berlin, by reason of the great number of Vessels that are seen constantly there, either going up or coming down, without reckoning the Boats of the City: for this River is join'd by an artificial Canal to the Oder, so that there is a free Navigation for small Craft, from Silesia across all Germany, till the Spré emtys it self into the Havel; and till this last flows at Havelberg into the Elb, wherby it communicates it self with the Ocean. With very little charge there might a Passage be made between the Oder and the Danube, at least a good part of the way; and the Land-Carriage of the rest wou'd signify little, the whole not exceeding twenty Leagues. Thus not only the Trade of Hungary might be carry'd on this way, but likewise of a good part of the Levant, besides many other Advantages; among which I reckon it not the least, that if by the Conjunction of France and Spain we shou'd com to be shut out of the Mediterranean Sea (which is a case I firmly trust will never happen) or that a Toll shou'd be exacted of all other Nations at the Strait's Mouth, like that of the King of Denmark on the Sound of the Baltic Sea, then the English and Dutch might bring home a great quantity of their Turky Merchandize by this Passage. I know the Remedy will be thought worse than the Disease, since the King of Prussia is not sole Master from the Danube to the Northern Ocean, and every great and petty Prince wou'd demand so many acknowlegements, as might not only much lessen the Profit but likewise prey upon the Stock. This is a Case that I hope will never need to be nicely examin'd, and my Design is only to indicat a Passage that may not yet be known to you, and so leave you to make what use of it you think fit. All the Dominions of his Prussian Majesty, as well inland as maritim, are excellently watered with navigable Rivers (which makes the Circulation, if not the Soul of Commerce) as the Rhine, the Maese, the Weser, the Elb, the Hagel, the Havel, the Werter, the Oder, the Vistula, the Pregel, and several others: besides that his Kingdom of Prussia, and his Dutchy of Pomerania, take up a great part of the Coast of the Baltic Sea, and ly extremely convenient for Traffick, as they drive a pretty considerable one, which by right management might be vastly improved.

10. BUT to return to Berlin, upon the Reparation of the Sluce (which I mention'd to you before) the King has caus'd a fine Medal to be struck, and likewise another to commemorat the Additions, Fortifications, and Ornaments, by which he has rendered this City remarkable, and to eternize the Arts and Commerce which he has therin so happily settl'd. I never saw a nobler Medal, than that which was struck on his taking upon him the Royal Title and Dignity; for 'tis a common mistake that the Emperor made him King, whatever Consent he might give together with other Princes, since in Prussia his Majesty is independent of all Power but that of God. The Reverse of this Medal is Justice crowning her self, with a Motto very proper for the Thing and the Occasion, *Suumcuique*, *To every*

Person his own. Another Medal I saw (wherof the Reverse is a HARPOCRATES) to denote the Zeal and Secrecy with which he assisted the Prince of Orange and the States of Holland in the Britannic Expedition, or in the late most glorious, seasonable, and never to be forgotten Revolution, which strictly intitles him to our Gratitude and Respect. There is also a Medal in Honor of the Prince Royal, and more than one for the Queen's Majesty; the Reverse of the last of which is a JUNO dandling a CUPID on her Knee, with these words,

In una sede morantur
Majestas & Amor.

that is,

Love and Majesty in one agree.

Here I take occasion, SIR, to tell you, that in this regard there is no Prince at present in Europe, who has a nobler and greater Soul than FREDERIC the ~~First~~third.[3] If the antient Romans cou'd return again to the World, they wou'd be amaz'd to find Barbarism overspread all their belov'd Italy, while the Arts and Sciences flourish in the midst of Germany, which in their time was little else but immense Forests and Marshes, the Receptacles of a savage and unpolish'd People, tho warlike, brave, and free. But above all they wou'd justly extol and admire the King of Prussia's Genius, who is inflam'd with those same refin'd Passions, that made or preserv'd the Glory of their own most celebrated Heroes. Like them he understands, he loves, he erects public Buildings, Statues, Aqueducts; he strikes Medals to celebrat the Occasion and to perpetuat the Example of Events; and makes significant Inscriptions every where, in imitation of those great Men. Such as dislike his Majesty's Conduct in som other matters (for what Prince is there exemt from Enemys or Detractors any more than privat Persons?) must needs in these things unwillingly commend him, because they are good in themselves, and notorious Facts known to so many as makes it impossible to conceal or deny them. There is yet another Statue of his Majesty actually preparing, which will be an extraordinary Piece of Workmanship. The Design is almost Gigantic, and it is to be the Ornament of a new Gate which will be call'd the Royal Gate, whence the Street is likewise to derive its Name. But another time I may send you a more ample Description of it, with the many Figures of Stone that are to embellish and accompany it.

11. IN the Quarter of Berlin, peculiarly so call'd, there is near the Wall of the Town a stately Amphitheatre for the fighting and baiting of Bears, Lions, Bulls, Urochsen which are the *Vri* of the Antients, and of other wild and fierce Beasts, of which a good Number is always kept underneath in their Dens. Tho the old Stables near the Palace are very large, yet he has built others in the new Town, which may be properly call'd magnificent, and are often mistaken by Strangers for som great Minister's Palace. They are divided into two Courts, and nine

Pavilions in equal distances. Over head is the Academy of the Painters, of the Learned, and of all the gentile Arts which are much incourag'd here; and there is likewise rais'd a conspicuous Observatory for Astronomers. This gave occasion to a Person, who had no great opinion of the Men of Letters in this Academy, to tell the King that he did very well to lodg his Horses and his Asses together. 'Tis for those Gentlemen so to distinguish themselves by their valuable Productions, as to make this Reflection to pass in the World for nothing but a Jest. Now of all the Curiositys of Berlin, the most principal is the new Royal Palace, which is a building and very forward in the Quarter of Colen, on the same Ground where the old Castle stood. I shall not enter into particulars, out of which I cou'd not extricat my self a long time; nor will I take this opportunity (tho a most proper one) to shew you my Skill in Architecture, and that I have read all the Commentators on VITRUVIUS. 'Tis better to say nothing on such a Subject, than not to say enough. But, till I can procure the Plan of it, I shall only inform you, that notwithstanding you have travel'd very far, yet you never saw any thing more exact, commodious, or stately; tho I confess you have bin in one or two that might be more capacious, but then they were less regular. In short, the other Palaces of Europe that have had so many Kings successively to inlarge, adorn, or repair them, are like to becom obscure, and to serve for a foil to that of the first Christian King of Prussia; as his very Crown and Scepter, by the Number, Splendor, and Value of their precious Stones, have already eclips'd all theirs. There are those who blame this Profusion of Diamonds, and think they might be better improv'd than thus to ly in dead stock: but tho the difference between Princes and privat Men be a sufficient Answer, yet 'tis not my business to enter into the Reasons of such things, but to give to you, SIR, a true Relation of Fact.

12. THE Citizens, in imitation of the Father of the Country, go on with new Buildings every day in all Quarters of the Town, each of 'em striving to outvy the rest; so that in a few Years Berlin will be one of the finest Citys that can be seen. Divers sorts of Manufactures are there in a most thriving Condition, as curious Works in Gold and Silver, in polish'd Steel and in Glass; as also light Stuffs, coarse Cloths, Stockins, with several other things. And really it cannot well be otherwise; for, besides the good Order, Justice, and Moderation, which I mention'd before as the natural and general Causes of these Effects, we ought not to forget three particular things that have highly contributed thereto. I give the first place to that great number of French Refugees, and other persecuted Protestants, who have found here a most assured Protection and Sanctuary, together with extraordinary Privileges and Immunitys, which must needs attract the favor of Heaven, as well as beget the temporal Consequences which naturally result from thence; for the more People, the more Consumtion and Commerce, and therfore the more Riches, Revenues, and Soldiers. This is so true, that

in the space of a few Years after this General Naturalization, the Incoms of the Post-Office, and all the several Excises, brought into the Treasury double what they us'd to do; the number of Houses increased prodigiously, and Bills of Exchange were much easier paid than formerly. At the beginning perhaps these things were little design'd, and Religion alone was the Motive; but once that the Consequences were perceiv'd, nothing has bin omitted to improve the Advantages, and som other Princes of Germany begin to follow the Example: but their Projects are sure to miscarry, if the Liberty and Privileges they give be not equal to those of the Natives here, or if they overcharge their Subjects or their Industry with Taxes when they find 'em begin to thrive. The Second thing is that intire Liberty of Conscience which all good Christians enjoy in this place, and throout all his Majesty's Territorys; which to the Inhabitants yields a secure and agreeable Dwelling, as it invites Strangers to settle among them, having nothing to fear about their Souls, no more than concerning their Bodys or Possessions. The Lutherans and the Calvinists live amicably together, notwithstanding the Efforts of designing Neighbors to break their Concord. Their Churches, I told you, were without all Marks of Distinction; and they are themselves indifferently prefer'd to Civil and Military Offices, according to their Merit or Recommendation, without any Brands of Infamy or Distrust on either side, to ~~hinder~~ further[4] and inlarge instead of lessening and healing their Breaches. Tho the King is himself a Calvinist, yet the National Religion in most of his Dominions is that of the Lutherans, and their Churches are paid by the Revenues appropriated to this purpose; while those of the Calvinists are supported by voluntary Contributions, excepting such as particularly belong to the Court. Yet in most Places the Calvinists have better Livings than the Lutherans; and since the Distinction is solely confin'd to the Clergy, without a Layman's getting or losing any thing in his Honor or Profit by professing either Religion, 'tis very probable that they have fewer Hypocrites than where it is beneficial or detrimental to be of a certain Sect: and there is Demonstration, that, supposing the Ministers of any side shou'd grow uneasy, they cou'd never draw the Laity into their Quarrel, who have already a full Liberty of worshipping God according to the Dictates of their Conscience; and in temporal Concerns they wou'd risk a certainty for an uncertainty, merely to gratify the Ambition of a Priest, which no wise Man will ever do, no more than any good Man can expect it. However the King omits nothing to unite all his Subjects, not by Incapacitys, Force, or Disgrace, but by Evangelical Persuasion, by the Tenderness of a common Father, and by representing the small Importance of their Differences. The Third and last thing is the great number of Houses which his Majesty builds in several Places for his own Use, but especially in the Neighborhood of Berlin, which makes an ample Compensation to this City for the barrenness of its Soil: and to these three Causes it is, that in a particular manner I attribute the sensible improvement of the Brandenburg Dominions and of the City of Berlin within the compass of a few Years.

13. I KNOW very well som Men of no contemtible Judgment are of Opinion, that it were more advisable not to build so many Houses, and to confine the Expence of them all to two or three, which wou'd render 'em more magnificent than those of any other German Prince. But besides that the King can furnish Mony enough to make two or three of his Houses as magnificent as he pleases (setting apart every Year, as he actually dos, 150000 Crowns towards his Buildings) his Subjects do likewise receive therby considerable Profits, both by their Labor, and by the Materials they furnish, for which they are punctually paid. This makes Mony circulat in the Country, and seems to be one of his Majesty's principal Views. There is not a Prince in the World, and it may be few privat Persons, that understands better than him the Charms and Pleasures of a Country Life; which were so much belov'd, prais'd, and cultivated by the great Men of Antiquity. This appears not only by the Time and Diversions he employs there, but likewise by the several Situations, the different Furniture, by the Distances and Structure of his Houses. They are most neatly kept, as becomes a Prince; and so compleatly provided according to their various Bulk or Uses, that nothing is ever removed from one House to another, each having whatever is fit for it self, without excepting even the Services of Gold and Silver Plate, which I am inform'd is a thing that

cannot be said of any other Prince in Europe. I shall now speak a word to you concerning each of these.

14. THE first I saw is Oranieburg,[5] begun by the late Elector for the Electress's Pleasure, call'd after the Name of her Family, and situated in a Country that much resembles Holland. There is near it a small City of the same Name, and all around are eternal Medows, water'd and divided by many Canals drawn out of the Hagel; and they are bounded by Woods, across which are cut several long Vistas, som of them reaching even to other Houses. It consists at present of two Courts, the Body of the House or the principal part being in the middle; his Majesty having augmented it by almost one half, and added several Ornaments to it in Honor of his Mother, as appears from a Latin Inscription that stands over the great Door. The Garden is very large, and furnish'd with Statues, Fountains, Obeliscs, Grottos, a Volery, an Orangery, and another little House some paces further call'd the Favorite, where the King may conveniently ly when he pleases. There is a Menagery a building, also a Hermitage, and all that depends on all these. The Spout in the great Stair-case mounts forty six foot, and is yet exceeded by another in the Garden, both being supply'd by most costly Water-works rais'd on the River-Side in a spacious Flat, where there is not the least Eminence to assist them. But the Gallery and Cabinet of Porcelain or China-Ware (containing likewise numberless Gems, antique Heads, Seals, and the like) is a Wonder that has not the like

elswhere. I don't believe the Emperor of China can show a greater Diversity, and he is the only Prince that can equal the Quantity. Nothing more agreeably entertains the Sight. The Order of 'em is admirable, and shows the methodical Genius of the King, who has rang'd them so finely in Pyramids, Obeliscs, Pillars, and into all the Forms and Figures conceivable, from the smallest Curiositys to Jarrs and other Vessels of a prodigious size. The Wainscot (if I may so call it) of these Rooms is of pure Looking-Glass, which by the Reflection of so many Raritys produces a charming Spectacle, the Moldings and Frames being exquisitly gilt and painted. From Berlin to this Place are four German Miles, distinguish'd by so many Pedestals of hewn Stone, with their proper Numbers and Inscriptions, in imitation of the milliary Stones of the antient Romans; but these last were erected| at the end of every thousand Paces.

15. THE same Distance and the same milliary Stones are found between Berlin and Postdam,[6] lying in an Island about four Leagues in Circumference, form'd by the Spré and the Havel. There is also here a Town of the same Name, environ'd with Hillocks, Coppicewoods, Groves, and Forests. One day it will be made a lovely Place, for the new Gate of a consummat Architecture will temt his Majesty to conform the rest of the House to it, tho at this present it be truly Royal. There is likewise a new Plan made for the Garden, and on the other side of the River they are contriving of

Cascades from a considerable Height over against the House, which seems to confirm my Prediction. A quarter of a League from thence there is a fine Menagery, where is kept the greatest number of Pheasants I ever saw. You see there many strange Birds, with other rare and exotic Animals: but the little Indian Goats, scarce bigger than our Rabbits, pleas'd me above all the rest. The Ile is diversify'd with thick Forests, flat Medows, and delightful Fields. About the middle of it stands the Pleasure-House and Garden of Bornheim, where grows the best Fruit of the Royal Gardens, as the King himself was pleas'd to tell me; for tho I went thither one Morning to view it, the Gardener did not vouchsafe to offer me as much as a Peach, but the complaints of every body else persuaded me it was no particular Slight. From a gentle Hill near that place you enjoy a most agreable Prospect from one end of the Iland to the other; you see the Conjunction of the two Rivers, and many Villages. Postdam[7] is almost mid-way between two lesser Houses belonging to his Majesty, well furnish'd as they are all, and very deliciously situated. Kapput being a small League lower, the River becoms much larger, and forms a sort of a Lake from thence to Postdam;[8] and tho Kleiniken be half a League higher towards Berlin, yet the River is there as large as at Kapput, by reason of the Confluence of several Waters, and the Division of the Spré and the Havel: so that the King may divert himself in his Yachts from Postdam[9] to either of these Houses as he finds himself dispos'd.

16. IN the Neighborhood of Berlin there are several other Houses, wherof I shall make no particular Description, as Faarlandt, Fridericsfeldt, Rosendaal, Keppenich, Rhudau, Blankenfeldt, Meyndershausen, Hoppengaarden, and Belvedere. 'Tis at Schoonhausen, within a League of Berlin, that the King dos ordinarily reside during the Summer-Season. The House is very convenient, the Gardens are handsom enough; and I have no where in Germany seen greener Borders, Walks, and Parterres. The King has yet several other Houses, as one at Tangermunden, and another lately built in the City of Magdenburg, facing the great Place before the Dome or Cathedral Church, and over against the Citadel, which is divided from it by the Elb. I have nothing to say about the Castle of Cleves, nor his Houses in Prussia, or in any of his other Dominions, where I have never bin; but of all these Places so commodious, or sumtuous, or agreable, the small House of Fridericsdaal, within a League of Oranieburg,[10] is the most to my fancy, as it is the most regularly built of all the rest, and after the Model of Marli, the King himself being the Architect. To retire with a select Company, or to be alone among variety of Books, Fridericsdaal is the Place I wou'd prefer before any other. Here the King is a Husbandman, having a mighty pretty Farm and a neat Dairy, manag'd by Suissers, who make as good Butter and Cheese as in their own Mountains. The Kitchin is furnish'd after the Dutch manner with Delfware. There is nothing more truly of a Country Tast; and I may justly say that all his Majesty's

Houses are each of them accommodated to som particular Pleasure's, to the several Seasons, or to different Scenes of Affairs.

17. THE Queen spends much of her Time in a Palace which is not yet finish'd on the Banks of the Spré, near the Village of Lutzelburg, whence it takes its Name, and within a little League of Berlin, from which you go to it all the way thro a Park,[11] and in a Treckschuit or Draw- boat by Water. Altho I speak of it after all the rest, yet it is far from being the last either in Capaciousness or Regularity, or Magnificence. The Garden, which lys between the House and the River, will be one of the finest (in proportion to its Extent) of all Germany, and it is not easily surpass'd already in your Country. But as nothing is yet brought to Perfection here, I shall not at present send you a more particular Description; tho there is no room to doubt but in a little time it will be a charming Place, under the direction of SOPHIA CHARLOTTE, the most beautiful Princess of her Time, and who is second to no Person in the Justness of her Thoughts, the Delicacy of Expressions, or the Graces of Conversation. Her Reading is infinit, and she is conversant in all manner of Subjects; nor is She more admir'd for her inimitable Wit, than for her exact Knowledg of the most abstruse parts of Philosophy: and (without flattering her high Dignity in the least) I must freely own that I never heard Objections more pertinently made, the Sophistry of an Argument quicker detected, nor either the difficulty or weakness of any

Opinion more easily penetrated by any other in my whole Life. No Body better understands the Art of giving an improving Relish to all Entertainments; but her favorit Diversion is Music, and one must judg as well of it as her Majesty (which is not easily don) to love it with a Passion equal to her's. She plays to Perfection on the Harpsichord, which she practises every day: she sings finely; and the famous BONONCINI, one of the greatest Masters alive, told me, that her Compositions are most exact. She loves to see Strangers, and to inform her self of all that's worthy or remarkable in their several Countrys; and she has so just an Idea of Government, that in all Germany they call her the Republican Queen. All that's gay and polite resort to her Court, where you may see a complete Harmony between what most of the World believe to be contrary if not extremes, I mean Learning and Mirth. As for her Person she's not very tall, but somwhat too plump: all her Features are extremely regular, her Complection fair and lively, her Eyes blue, and her Hair Cole-black. She loves to have handsom Women about her, and most of her Maids of Honor are such. The Prince Royal her only Child (for the Princess Royal, marry'd to the Hereditary Prince of Hesse-Cassel, the King had by his first Wife of the House of Bareith) the young Prince, I say, is lodg'd in an Apartment of the Palace at Berlin, and has yet no House for himself but Wosterhausen for hunting. Nature has join'd to the Masculin Air of the future Hero, all the Beauty and Modesty of Virgins; for he is truly a most lovely Prince, very mild and affable, having a good Understanding, curious to know every thing, and not without Application to his Studys under Count DHONA, who is his Governor. I often saw him ride the great Horse, and perform his other Exercises with great Approbation. He's rather too low for his Age, and inclin'd to be fat, tho very proper in all his make; but provided he be preserv'd from the Contagion of Flatterers, and such other Corrupters of young Princes, it matters not much for a shape. His Name is FREDERIC WILLIAM, and he begins his fifteenth Year, as the King dos his forty sixth, and the Queen is about ending her thirty fourth, being * born the second of October, N.S. 1668.

18. BEFORE I quite leave the Article of Houses, I must tell you, that when I went to Stettin in the Swedish Pomerania, I paid my duty to Prince PHILIP the King's next Brother, at his House in Schwedt upon the Oder, where I staid several days. 'Tis a sweet place, not only from the Neighborhood of so large a River, but likewise for all sorts of Game. The Prince himself is a well timber'd Man, full of Goodness, and generally belov'd; and his Princess, who is Cousin German to our late King WILLIAM being Sister to the present Prince of Anhalt-Dessau,[12] is a Woman of great Beauty, of an affable Disposition, ingaging in Conversation, and adorn'd with many excellent Qualitys, as well as happy in a

---

**But this brightest ornament of her sex is lately dead, and those, who had the opportunity to know her true worth, will forever mourn her loss.*

numerous Issue. I shall always remember with becoming Respect and Gratitude the Favors I receiv'd from their Highnesses; and I shall deeply retain the Impressions of that place, because, altho it be a Court, yet 'tis a pleasant Country retirement, for which sort of Life I ever had a strong Inclination, but not to be there alone. The King's other Brothers are the Markgraves ALBERT and CHRISTIAN, and his only Sister is Dutchess Dowager of Courland, whose Son, the present Duke, is, during the lamentable distress of his Country, entertained by the King his Uncle. 'Tis at Berlin that his Prussian Majesty dos commonly keep his Court, especially in Winter. It is very numerous and magnificent. Every thing shines with Gold, Silver, and Jewels. The Equipages are sumtuous, the Courtiers well bred, and obliging to Strangers, in all things they do honor to their Master and show themselves deserving of their several Posts. Som of the foren Ministers pretend that they overdo in the finery of their Habits and in the expensiveness of public Festivals; but whether they have Reason or Envy of their side, I shall not take upon me to judg. I can tell you in general that the King must needs be well serv'd, not merely because he employs the ablest Persons he can find, but by the fundamental Maxim of regulating his Affairs: for 'tis his pleasure that every Man shou'd not only faithfully acquit himself of his Commission, but that he confine and acquit himself wholly to that, without forming any Cabals and privat Intrigues, or at all intermeddling in other Peoples Business. As for his Troops, we have had both in the last and present War signal Proofs of what they are capable to do; and no Man is more convinced, or a better Judg of it than you. Those who continue here, and whom I saw pass in a Review before the King, are handsom robust Fellows, with Arms and Clothing to which no Exceptions can be made, no more than to their Disciplin and Exercise, as som experienced Generals inform'd me. The Troops that are in Prussia are much commended, as also those in the Service of the Emperor, whose Number and Condition you have learn'd from your Resident Monsieur de MORTAGNE my very good Friend.

19. NOW among all my Observations in this Country, what charm'd me most is the new Regulation of the Militia, an Enterprise worthy of the Count of WARTEMBERG, who inspir'd it into his Royal Master, and 'tis begun to be executed with much Success. They are frequently taught their Exercise in the Parishes by Veteran Soldiers, more rarely but often enough elswhere in formed Bodys; and the King himself gives them Ammunition-Coats the first Year, the Subjects being oblig'd to furnish themselves ever after, in consideration of which there will be som abatement of their Imposts. I had the Honor to follow the King to Oranieburg,[13] when he treated his most illustrious Mother in Law, the presumtive Successor of our English Crown, her Royal Highness SOPHIA, the Electress Dowager of Hanover, who coms generally every Summer to pass som Time with the Queen her Daughter, as the latter goes in Carnaval-time to her native City of Hanover,

for which she retains a cordial Affection. His Majesty receiv'd the Electress coming out of her Coach, under the Discharge of thirty six Pieces of Cannon, four and twenty Trumpets sounding, two Pair of Kettle-Drums, and I know not how many Hautboys. There were three Companys drawn up before the Gate, of which two belong'd to this new Militia, having grey Coats lin'd with Orange, and were not thought inferior to the regular Troops in handling their Arms. You know, SIR, that during King WILLIAM's Life I publish'd a Treatise, entitul'd *The Militia Reform'd*, with this very View, showing how all our Country, and specially our Garrisons, wou'd not only be secure during the absence of our regular Troops, but that in case of need we might recruit or reinforce them by som of these: wheras such Princes as have but their ordinary Troops, are in danger of being ruin'd by the loss of one Battel, not being in a Condition for a long time to bring such another Army into the Field; while those who exercise their Militia have perpetual Resources of able Men, who already understand the Theory, and will quickly learn the Practice, as I have prov'd by the Examples of the antient Greecs and Romans. We are not ignorant that the victorious Troops of the King of Sweden, and the inexhaustible Levys of Suisserland, are a real Country Militia, kept in continual Exercise with a very little Trouble and Charge. When our Kings had in View the setting up of Popery and Arbitrary Tower, the Court oppos'd all Projects or Overtures for arming the People. Since King WILLIAM re-establish'd our sinking

Liberty, those who were discontented with that or him, wou'd not consent to arm so many for their Defence. And, to let you see that I am not partial (as you somtimes reproach me) to any sort of People som of our Country Gentlemen understood this matter so little, that they were against it from such pitiful reasons as I shou'd be asham'd to relate, if in the House of Commons, on occasion of a Bill for regulating the Militia, they had not spoke them too publickly to be kept a secret. Their First Reason was the Preservation of the Game, as if those who did not regard the Laws to that purpose, wou'd scruple to get them Guns when they meant to transgress; or as if the People of England were rather to be expos'd to their Enemys, than a few Beasts and Birds to them: besides that the King of Prussia has vastly a greater store of Game, and yet trusts to the Orders he has made to secure it. Their Second Reason was the fear of increasing Robbers or House-breakers; but in effect if they do not put Arms into the Hands of all such (for they'll take care to provide themselves) yet they disarm innocent People, who will yield Obedience to the Laws, and so be made incapable of self-defence: wheras had every Man a Gun, they wou'd not only deter Rogues from assaulting them, but they cou'd com seasonably to the Rescue and Assistance of their Neighbors. These and such other Reasons might temt a Man to believe, that they who made use of them, had som dangerous Design in their Heads; but that their other Actions prove 'em uncapable of it, and therfore I am persuaded that in this matter they sincerely meant what they spoke, as much as they, who, out of a pretended Zeal for the establish'd Church, were against arming the Dissenters, who are as hearty against France as themselves. But to return to the King of Prussia's Militia, the Denomination of the Regiments will be taken from the great Citys and Provinces, which will breed an Emulation among those Troops to equal or excede one another, for the Honor of their Country: and I verily believe, the King of France had the same Thoughts, when he followed the same Method, in the Names of several of his standing Regiments. I shall only add on this Subject, that those who do not see with a good Ey the aggrandizing of the House of Brandenburg, make as if they thought lightly of all this, altho to little purpose: for such is his Majesty's Resolution, that he will not be easily put out of conceit with a Project which is likely one Day to contribute so much to the Wealth and Safety of the Country, as well, as to the Glory and Power of the Prince, who has nothing to fear, so long as he procures the Good of the People committed by God to his charge.

30.[14] I KNOW I cou'd not send more agreable News to one, who bears so much Respect and good Will to the King of Prussia, not without the strongest Reasons in the World: for besides that on many Accounts the States will have perpetual need of his Friendship, Counsels, and Assistance, as his Majesty reciprocally of theirs, your Interests being inseparable; I can also say of my own certain Knowlege, that no one Person whatever either in

England or Holland appears to have a deeper Sense and Apprehension of the overgrown Power of France with its pernicious Consequences. This makes him heartily zealous for the common Cause, as none has more at heart the Prosperity of the Protestant Religion, on all which Accounts he'll ingage as far as any Prince in maintaining the Liberty of Europe. His Majesty has more than once condescended to discourse me on these Subjects; his Excellency the Count of WARTEMBERG has frequently entertained me to the same purpose: and tho I am in no public Station, yet I cannot but gladly imbrace an Opportunity of communicating to you those Dispositions so favorable to your own Country as well as to mine. The King has given a late Instance of this, which I mention by reason of certain scandalous Reports that were wickedly spread in the World by malicious People. What advantageous Offers did he generously refuse from the French, at that very time when they were at his Gates, and ravaging his Dutchy of Cleves? This was so far from shaking him, as they vainly imagin'd, that on the contrary, as well by his Resolution in advising the continuing of the Siege, as by the Valor of his Troops, and the Ammunition which he lent you, he contributed more than all the other Princes of the Empire to humble France by the taking of Keyserswaardt, when so many were of opinion to abandon it, which wou'd have begun a Campaign I shou'd be sorry to describe. To enter into the Character of any Persons besides the Royal Family was no part of your Instructions: and as to certain other matters you must have som regard to my particular Circumstances; but if I live, you may one time or other receive larger Memoirs. In the mean while I continue,

SIR,

Your most oblig'd

and obedient Servant,

TOLAND.

AN
ACCOUNT
OF THE
Court of Hanover,
SENT FROM
Berlin to the Hague,
September 23. *N.S.* 1702.

SIR,

1. SINCE you are pleas'd to say, that my Relation of this Court was not unacceptable to you, I take the greater Courage to send the Account you desire of the Court of Hanover; tho I cannot but be sensibly concerned, and in som Confusion, when I appear in this manner before a Person that's accustom'd to receive Dispatches from abler Hands. In my way from Holland to that Place a Year ago, there occur'd nothing remarkable, but between this City and Hanover I was much affected with a very mournful Spectacle; for if we cannot help being touched at the Sight of a Skeleton or dead Carcase, how much more

must we be mov'd at the Ruins of a populous, large, and free City? Brunswick, you know, not many Years ago, was one of the Imperial or Hans-Towns. During the time it continu'd a Republic it flourish'd exceedingly, drove a mighty Trade, and had a Bank of sufficient Credit. But the Dukes of Brunswick renewing their Pretensions upon it, which it seems were very just, they took it in a few Days, having borrowed first all the Pouder in the Town for another pretended Expedition, whence a Brunswicker became a Name of Reproach in the other Imperial Citys. Immediatly all the wealthy Merchants transported themselves, and what they cou'd of their Effects, to Hamburgh, Amsterdam, and other trading Towns; the Bank was vanish'd in an instant, never to be reviv'd (for 'tis a sort of Plant, that cannot live an hour, in arbitrary Ground) and all things went to Rack and Desolation. The Dukes of Wolfembuttle do now possess the same extent of Walls, and possibly the same number of Streets, but not a twentieth part of the Inhabitants, and I may say not a hundredth part of the Wealth. A vast many Houses are without any Dwellers at all; and others, that belong'd to rich Merchants, have som poor Devils living in the Ground-floors, while stately Apartments, with spacious Courts, Warehouses, and other Offices, stand emty, or are fill'd with Hops, or Corn, or Straw, or somthing of that kind. There are very few substantial Men left, and very little Business; but least of all in their annual Fairs, which are still kept up, and serve for merry Meetings to the neighboring Princes and Nobility. The City is divided into five Wards, each of which had its proper Hall, besides the common Town-House. Now, one of those public Buildings is turn'd into a Flesh-market; another I saw fill'd with Hops, which is a great Commodity here by reason of their Mum; and the chief of all is most naturally transformed into an Opera-house: for when a free City falls under the Dominion of an arbitrary Prince, the likeliest use for its Guild-hall is to becom either a Playhouse or a Court of Guard. I din'd there with som Officers, and ask'd them the reason, as a Stranger, how that Town, which appeared to have once made a nobler Figure, fell in so small time to decay. One of 'em told me the Citizens were a Pack of Rogues that deserv'd no better, and that they were never good Subjects till they were made poor; which is, as I understood it, that formerly they were willing to keep their own, but that now they had nothing to strive for. Another in the Company, who had som Imployment, and pretended to Politics, said that it was very true they were downright Cheats, for that when the Town was taken, there was little Mony found in their Bank (a woful disappointment!) so that they dealt upon imaginary Credit. I answer'd, that when they understood the Designs against them, they might probably convey the Mony to other Places; or granting their Effects were not answerable to their Credit, that this was common to them with most others, it being never suppos'd that all who deal with any will make their Demands at once. This I cou'd never make him conceive, and when he told me that the Prince gave them Time to satisfy their Creditors, but that they cou'd never hitherto do it, I answer'd him that it was then too late, since their Union subsisted no longer, however they might still bear the same Name; nor did I question but in this Dispersion, where every Man shifted for himself, there was fraud enough practis'd, tho as a public Body they might all be very honest: for such is the nature of Mankind, who are much beholding to equal Laws and prudent Regulations.

2. IT is surprizing, SIR, to consider how little Trade is understood in most parts of Germany, and how few in the Service of Princes are Masters of political Arithmetic. A very few they are indeed that have any tolerable skill in Figures or Calculations, which proves a notable Injury to the Exchequer, and generally occasions the Prince to be the Dupe of all Undertakers or Farmers of any public Dutys, and to be impos'd upon in Treatys with foren States. But I beg your pardon for this Digression, occasion'd by my Conversation in Brunswick. Last Year I spent five or six Weeks in Hanover, when the Earl of MACCLESFIELD came there from the King of England with the Act of Succession pass'd in our Parliament the preceding Winter, and wherby in default of Issue of the Queen's Body, the Princess SOPHIA, and her Descendents being Protestants are to succede to the Imperial Crown of England, France, and Ireland. I had then all imaginable Opportunitys to make Observation on the Court, and to understand the Characters of Persons. But as for the Elector's Country, I have seen little of it besides Hanover

itself; tho you may perceive by the Map that it is of a considerable extent, which will yet be greatly augmented when the Dutchy of Zell is united to it after the present Duke's decease, who is very old. All in Office under the Duke have already sworn conditional Allegiance to the Elector, nor is there any thing of moment transacted there without his Privity and Consent. He and the Duke have the same public Ministers in foren Courts, which shows them to be in the same Secret or Interest: and in a word, all things are so well adjusted, that there can be no Impediments to the peaceable enjoyment of that Succession, how industriously soever som, who are not well wishers to that Family, have bin laboring (as they still continue) to make it a Subject of Contest and Division. Another Argument of the goodness of the Elector's Dominions is the greatness of his Revenue, which is about 300000 Pounds Sterling, without reckoning the Addition that will be made by the Dutchy of Zell. We may judg likewise by the Quota of Troops he furnishes to the Empire, those he lets out to the Allys, and those he keeps on foot at home, the number of all which you know already, and that his Highness draws a mighty Profit from his Silver Mines in the Hartz or part of the Hercynian Forest, at the Foot of the high Mountain *Melibocus*, call'd at present Bokkenberg,[15] mentioned by PTOLOMEY, and was the Country of the German Hero ARMINIUS or HARMAN. And lastly 'tis no small Benefit to that Family, that the Bishopric of Osnabrug falling by turns to Protestants and Papists, the Bishop of the latter Persuasion may be chosen without Restriction among all the qualify'd Persons of his Communion, wheras in the Protestant Turn it must be always one of the House of Hanover. This makes them with very good reason look upon that City and Bishopric as part of their Territorys, and therfore they are more careful of it, and less exacting on the Subjects, than where Clergymen possess only for their Lives, and are willing to make the best of the present, without any regard to the good of their Successors. By the way, their Relation to this Bishopric has bin made the Ground of a base Calumny, by som of their ill wishers in England; and 'tis mention'd in many of their Pamphlets, as if they were so indifferent in point of Religion, as generally to breed up, one of their Sons a Papist in order to qualify him for Bishop of Osnabrug: and people not knowing but the Bishop of Osnaburg is always a Papist, because at present he is so, being the Duke of LORAIN's Brother, and hearing likewise that several of the House of Hanover have bin actually Bishops there; they too easily suffer themselves to be abused by the falsest Fact in the World.

3. HANOVER is situated in a sandy Soil upon the River Laine, which is navigable only by small Boats. It is regularly fortify'd, and divided into the new and old Towns, which is always a sign of a thriving place. The Apartments of the Palace are very fine, and richly furnish'd. It was in the old Time a large Monastery, but so well metamorphos'd since, that no Footsteps remain of the Original. There is a pritty Theatre with handsom Lodges[16] for all Qualitys; for

no body pays Mony that goes to a Play there, the Prince, as in som other Courts of Germany, being at all the expence to entertain the Town as well as the Court. But the Opera-house in the Castle is visited as a Rarity by all Travellers, as being the best painted and the best contrived in all Europe. The Elector's Chappel is also finely painted, and certainly nothing can be in greater Order and Method than whatever belongs to his Highness, as I shall tell you more particularly by and by. The Court in general is extremely polite, and even in Germany it is accounted the best, both for Civility and Decorum. The Vice of Drinking (for which that Nation is so much branded) is so far from reigning here, that tho no body is abridged of his Pleasure in this respect, yet I never knew greater Sobriety nor a more exact Government in a privat Family. It is not for me to pretend to judg of their Entertainments. Strangers of Figure or Quality are commonly invited to the Elector's Table, where they are amaz'd to find such easy Conversation, and to be allow'd a Liberty that no body who deserves it will abuse. At Court-hours all People of Fashion meet there without any manner of constraint; and provided they know what difference to make between Men and Things (which everybody that coms there is suppos'd to-do) they may freely talk of any Subject even with the Elector himself. The Ladys are perfectly well bred, obliging, and many of 'em handsom. Madam de KILMANSEGG, Daughter to the Count of PLATA, may pass for a Woman of Sense and Wit, and her Sister-in-Law the young Countess of Plata may pass for a Beauty, in any Court whatsoever. The Electress's Maids of Honor are worthy of the Rank they enjoy, especially Mademoiselle SCHULENBURG, who in the Opinion of others as well as mine is a Lady of extraordinary Merit. All the Gentlemen that belong to their Highnesses are, as far as ever I cou'd judg, Persons of Worth and Ability. I need not inform you that the Count of PLATA is first Minister, and that the Baron de GORITZ is not better known to you for an able Statesman, than he is to me for a Man of excellent Parts and great Generosity. The Chancellor Monsieur HUGO is a Man of good Learning, and bears much such a Character there for a most capable, intrepid, and uncorrupted judg, as my Lord Chief Justice HOLT dos in England. That they want not Men of Letters, I need but name Monsieur LEIBNITZ for an Example, who is here a Privy Counsellor and an Assistant in the Court of Chancery, but better known in the Commonwealth of Learning by his Discoverys in the Mathematics, and by his *Codex Diplomaticus*, which shows that he's equal to the Task he has undertaken, I mean, of writing the History of the most Serene House of Brunswick and Lunenburg. I cannot agree to his metaphysical Notions, but possibly my own Apprehension may be in fault; and if I name no other Persons on this occasion, 'tis not that they are unworthy your notice, but that I had not your Commands for doing it. Only I shou'd be a very ill Judg as well as very ungrateful, if I made no mention of the Baron de BRAUN, one of the Electress Dowager's Gentlemen, a Saxon by Birth, a Man of good Learning and better Judgment; he's truly faithful to the Interest of his Mistriss, a Lover of the English Nation, and one of the most observing, tho not the most talkative of the Court.

4. THE National Religion of the Elector's Dominions is the Lutheran, tho the Calvinists and all other Persuasions are perfectly easy, and enjoy a complete Liberty of Conscience; Favor and Preferments being confer'd indifferently on all good Protestants. The Electress has built a pritty Church in the new Town for the French Refugees, and our late King was a liberal Benefactor to it. Tho her Royal Highness be a Calvinist, and might chuse to have none but such about her Person, yet most of her Women and other immediat Servants are Lutheran; as the Elector, who is of this last Persuasion, has many Calvinists belonging to him: and both their Highnesses, to show a good Example, and their unfeign'd Charity in these lesser Differences, do often go to Church together; neither was any of their Followers ever known to scruple accompanying 'em to either place, nor is there any manner of dispute or dislike among them on this account. I beg your pardon, SIR, for using the Words Calvinist and Lutheran, as if the Authority of MARTIN LUTHER or JOHN CALVIN were the Ground of any Man's Religion. The Language of Germany is Evangelic and Reform'd, but I adapt my Expressions to the Dialect of other Places. Since the Reformation no public Body of Men have manifested a greater degree of Moderation than the Clergy of this

Country, as being seconded and influenc'd by the best and wisest Race of Princes that have bin known to reign any where, which is no more than I often heard their Enemys allow. The celebrated CALIXTUS, who endeavor'd so much the Union of both the Partys, was a Professor in the University of Helmstadt, belonging to the House of Brunswick: and most of the Clergy are Syncretists, as they call those who admit both to Communion. The Protestant Abbot (or rather Warden of a College) MOLANUS, has often assur'd me, that he wou'd readily communicat with the Church of England, with whose Service he is well acquainted. He is a Man of no mean Literature, a curious Collector of natural Raritys, and has besides many antient the best Collection that can be seen of modern Medals, consisting of entire Sets of most Princely Houses in Europe, and the greatest part of them Gold and Silver, which amounts to a mighty Sum. Both the Princes and People cannot forbear admiring how we in England can keep up our Divisions about matters of much less Importance, or that, we cannot differ without so much Rancor; and Virulence as we commonly show in Words and Actions against one another. The Lutherans of Saxony, of Denmark, Sweden, and som other Places, are of quite another Spirit, and more rigid, if possible, than the Papist themselves, wherof I shall give you the true Reasons another time. The Clergy seldom appear at Court either at Hanover or Berlin; and it wou'd be no less scandalous for their Characters to be seen solliciting there for Preferments, than if in your Country they went to Taverns or Coffee-houses, which is as great a disgrace as if in England they frequented the Theatre or other Houses of worse fame.

5. YOU may be sure, SIR, that the Earl of MACCLESFIELD's Reception at the Court of Hanover was extraordinary magnificent, and that a Person who came on his Errand must needs be very welcome. You desire an Account of it, and this I take to be a proper Place. He bore no particular Character, but was sent by the King with the Act of Succession, both to grace it with a Man of that Quality, and as his Father bore a Relation to the Queen of BOHEMIA's Court, as well as for being one of the heartiest Persons alive for the Thing he went about. And in Justice to his Memory, I am oblig'd to tell you, that notwithstanding he was ordinarily a Man of little Ceremony among his Friends, yet that none cou'd behave himself more handsomly on this Occasion, that none cou'd do greater Honor to his King and Country in executing his Commission, and that he so well approved himself in all Respects to their Highnesses and the whole Court, that they exceeded in esteem for his Person what they ow'd to the Minister of a Prince they had in so high a Veneration, and to whom they were, and thought themselves so signally oblig'd. He was received by Deputys of the best Quality on the Frontiers of the Country, and his Expences were defrayed on the Road with all his Retinue, till he arriv'd at Hanover. There one of the largest Houses in the whole City was assign'd for his Entertainment, and to lodg as many of the

Gentlemen that accompany'd him as he wou'd please to have near him, the rest being dispos'd into other Houses of the Neighborhood at the Elector's Charge. During all the time of his stay, not only between thirty and forty Gentlemen who came along with him, but likewise all Englishmen that pass'd that way, were treated on free cost. It was a continu'd Feasting, and I do not exceed when I say, that the two great Tables kept in this English Hotel were as plentifully and as sumtuously furnish'd the last Day as the first. All the Servants had half a Crown a Day given 'em in good Silver Pieces to provide for themselves; for they wou'd not disgrace 'em, it seems, with their Master's broken Meat, nor be at the trouble to dress for them in particular. The Citizens had Orders, which they observ'd, not to take any thing for Meat and Drink of any English~~man~~,[17] if his humor shou'd lead him to desire it, The Elector's own Servants waited on them every Morning with Silver Coffee and Tea-pots to their Chambers. Burgundy, Champaigne, Rhenish, and all manner of Wines were as common as Beer. A number of Coaches and Chairs were appointed to bring 'em every Day to Court, to carry 'em back to their Lodgings, and to go whither-soever else they wou'd. They were entertained with Music, Balls, and Plays; and every Person made it his Business to oblige them. There was a very fine Ball, and a splendid appearance of Ladys, the Evening after my Lord deliver'd the Act of Succession to the Electress. His Lordship did often eat at the Electoral Table, and som of the Gentlemen were always there in their Turns. They were frequently entertained by the Ministers of State; and if any of 'em (as I know of none) did misbehave himself, it cou'd not well be otherwise among so many young People; and I defy the like number, unless they shou'd be pick'd on purpose, to carry themselves more decently. Most of 'em met together by chance in Holland, and the half of 'em did not com in his Lordship's Train out of England.

6. AFTER som days he went to Zell to wait on the Duke, and from thence took a Turn to Hamburgh, where he was treated and made free by the English Company. He soon return'd again to Hanover, and when the Time was com for his departure, he was presented by her Royal Highness with her own Picture set in Diamonds, and the Electoral Crown of the same Materials over it, to the value of several thousand Pounds. The Elector's Present was a huge Bason and Ewer of Massy Gold to a very considerable value; and the Duke of Zell gave him a great many Gold Medals, to dispose of at his pleasure. Mr. KING the Herald, who brought the Garter to his Electoral Highness, tho his Lordship performed the Ceremony, was nobly presented. A Present was likewise given to the Reverend Doctor SANDYS, his Lordship's Chaplain, who had the Honor to preach, and read the Common Prayers of the Church of England before the Electress in her Anti-Chamber. She made the Responses, and perform'd the Ceremonys as punctually as if she had bin us'd to it all her Life; for she ever had our

Liturgy by her, tho I believe this was the first time that it was publicly read at Hanover, for which reason many assisted who understood not a tittle of it. Her Royal Highness approves it highly, tho she has not set it up in her own Chappel (as som uneasy Spirits wou'd have her) lest she shou'd seem to intimat, as she said, that she was before of a different Religion, when 'tis but the National Establishment of England. A Present was also given to Mr. WILLIAMS his Lordship's Secretary; and what Marks of Favor their Highnesses were pleased to confer on my self, I pretend not to have deserv'd by any Services I cou'd render their Family, nor on any personal Account. The Present was partly in Gold Medals; but what I much esteem, and will always preserve, is the Queen of Prussia, the Electress, the Elector, and the young Prince's Pictures done in Oil Colors, and very like. My Lord Viscount SEA and SEAL, my Lord MOHUN, and my Lord TUNBRIGE, were treated as became their Quality, and with particular Kindness and Confidence, as Persons that were sincerely devoted to the Family: and because when my Lord MOHUN was very young, and not capable to distinguish his Company, he had the misfortune to commit som Excesses, I am glad to be able to tell you, SIR, of, my own Knowlege, that none of the Company was more generally acceptable, that none liv'd with greater Sobriety, nor delivered himself on all Occasions with better Judgment or in politer Language; and he still continues to convince the World of his Reformation, as he is like to prove an Ornament to the Upperhouse of Parliament. Captain TYRREL, Mr. GODFREY, and Sir ANDREW FOUNTAIN were distinguish'd by the Electress, and I am confident every body must needs have gon away perfectly satisfy'd with their Reception, and with all the People of the Place; for they had many Opportunitys of getting good Acquaintance, by reason that som of the best Fashion always din'd with my Lord. You were at Loo, I remember, when he returned, and gave an Account of his Negotiation to the King, who was wonderfully pleas'd with the Success of his own Work. There he presented me to kiss his Majesty's Hand, and took off those Impressions which might have bin made upon him, by som of them who endeavor'd to prepossess him against those that were the most zealous for his Service, and the most faithful in his Interests. My Lord himself went with a prejudice against me to Hanover, where he was throly undeceiv'd, and became my hearty Patron, till just on his going home he was remov'd by Death from the Service of his Country and his Friends.

7. HAVING thus describ'd my Lord MACCLESFIEID's Reception, I com now to what you gave me most in charge, the Characters of the chiefest Persons of the Electoral Family, wherin I shall be very fair and exact. I need not tell you, what everybody knows, that the Electress Dowager, the Princess SOPHIA, is Daughter to the unfortunat King of Bohemia by the Princess ELIZABETH, only Daughter to our King JAMES the First: and had this last asserted the Cause of his Son-in-Law with that Vigor and Heartiness

that the Nation press'd him to do, and not so unpoliticly or rather unnaturally abandoned him, out of his desire of the Spanish Match, or from som worse Designs, his Posterity had in all probability reign'd to this day on the Throne of Bohemia. The Electress is three and seventy Years of Age, which she bears so wonderfully well, that had I not many Vouchers, I shou'd scarce dare venture to relate it. She has ever enjoy'd extraordinary Health, which keeps her still very vigorous, of a cheerful Countenance, and a merry Disposition. She steps as firm and erect as any young Lady, has not one Wrinkle in her Face which is still very agreable, nor one Tooth out of her Head, and reads without Spectacles, as I often saw her do Letters of a small Character in the dusk of the Evening. She's as great a Worker as our late Queen, and you cannot turn your self in the Palace without meeting som Monuments of her Industry, all the Chairs of the Presence-Chamber being wrought with her own Hands. The Ornaments of the Altar in the Electoral Chappel are all of her Work. She bestow'd the same favor on the Protestant Abby or College of Lockum, with a thousand other Instances fitter for your Lady to know than for your self. She's the most constant and greatest Walker I ever knew, never missing a Day, if it proves fair, for one or two hours, and often more, in the fine Garden of Hernhausen, of which I shall speak before I have finish'd. She perfectly tires all those of her Court that attend her in that Exercise, but such as have the Honor to be entertained by her in Discourse. She has bin long admir'd by all the

Learned World, as a Woman of incomparable Knowlege in Divinity, Philosophy, History, and the Subjects of all sorts of Books, of which she has read a prodigious quantity. She speaks five Languages so well, that by her Accent it might be a Dispute which of 'em was her first. They are Low-Dutch, German, French, Italian, and English, which last she speaks as truly and easily as any Native; which to me is matter of amazement, whatever advantages she might have in her Youth by the Conversation of her Mother: for tho the late King's Mother was likewise an Englishwoman of the same Royal Family, tho he had bin more than once in England before the Revolution, tho he was marry'd there, and his Court continually full of many of that Nation, yet he cou'd never conquer his foren Accent. But indeed the Electress is so intirely English in her Person, in her Behavior, in her Humor, and all her Inclinations, that naturally she cou'd not miss of anything which peculiarly belongs to our Iland. She was ever glad to see Englishmen, long before the Act of Succession. She professes to admire our Form of Government, and understands it mighty well; yet she asks so many Questions about Familys, Customs, Laws, and the like, as sufficiently demonstrat her profound Wisdom and Experience. She has a due Veneration (as I told you before) for the Church of England, without losing Affection or Charity for any other sort of Protestants; and appears charm'd with the moderat Temper of our present Bishops and others of our learned Clergy, especially for their Approbation of the Liberty establish'd by Law to

Protestant Dissenters. She's ador'd for her Goodness among the Inhabitants of the Country, and gains the Hearts of all Strangers by her unparallel'd Affability. No Distinction is ever made in her Court concerning the Partys into which Englishmen are divided, and wherof they carry the Effects and Impressions with them whithersoever they go, which makes others somtimes uneasy as well as themselves. There it is enough that you be an Englishman, nor can you ever discover by your Treatment which are better lik'd, the Whigs or the Torys: these are the Instructions given to all the Servants, and they take care to execute them with the utmost exactness. I was the first who had the Honor of kneeling and kissing her Hand on account of the Act of Succession; and she said, among other Discourse, that she was afraid the Nation had already repented their Choice of an old Woman, but that she hop'd none of her Posterity wou'd give them any Reasons to grow weary of their Dominion, I answer'd, that the English had too well consider'd what they did to change their Minds so soon, and that they still remember'd they were never so happy as when they were last under a Woman's Government. Since that Time, SIR, we have a further Confirmation of this Truth by the glorious Administration of Queen ANNE. The Electress is but lately return'd from this Court to Hanover; she still continues in perfect Health, and may she do so many Years!

8. THE Elector GEORGE LEWIS was born the 28th of May N.S. 1660. He's a proper, middle-siz'd, well-

proportion'd Man, of a gentile Address, and good Appearance. He's not addicted much to any Diversions besides Hunting; is reserv'd, and therfore speaks little, but judiciously. He's not to be exceeded in his Zeal against the intended universal Monarchy of France, and so is most hearty for the common Cause of Europe, wherin his own is so necessarily involved. He understands our Constitution the best of any Forener I ever knew; and tho he be well vers'd in the Art of War, and of invincible Courage, having often expos'd his Person to great Dangers in Hungary, ~~in the Morea~~,[18] on the Rhine, and in Flanders (of which you cannot be ignorant) yet he's naturally of peaceable Inclinations, which mixture of Quality's is agreed by the Experience of all Ages to make the best and most glorious Princes. He's a perfect Man of Business, exactly regular in the Oeconomy of his Revenues, reads all Dispatches himself at first hand, writes most of his own Letters, and spends a very considerable part of his Time about such Occupations in his Closet, and with his Ministers. I hope therfore that none of our Countrymen will be so injudicious as to think his Reserv'dness the Effect of Sullenness or Pride, nor mistake that for State which really proceeds from Modesty, Caution, and Deliberation: for he's very affable to such as accost him, and expects that others shou'd speak to him first, which is the best Information I cou'd have from all about him, and I partly know to be true by Experience. And as to what I said of his Frugality in laying out the public Mony, I need not give a more particular Proof, than that all the Expences of his Court (as to Eating, Drinking, Fire, Candles, and the like) are duly paid every Saturday Night; the Officers of his Army receive their Pay every Month, as likewise his Envoys in every part of Europe; and all the Officers of his Houshold, with the rest that are on the Civil List, are clear'd off every half Year. His Administration is most equitable, mild, and prudent. He's the most belov'd by his Subjects of any Prince in the World. There is no Division or Faction among them, by reason of his impartial Favor; and instead of railing or grumbling against his Person, they wou'd never make an end (if you wou'd have patience to listen) of telling Storys denoting his Justice and Moderation, particularly in Disputes about the Titles of Land, or any other Cause depending between him and his Subjects. He understands English, and in a little time will speak it readily. He spends much of his Time at Hernhausen, which is a Country-house about an English Mile and a half from Hanover. The Garden is delicat indeed, the Water-works great and noble, the Basins and Fountains extremely large, the Wilderness curiously contrived, and deck'd with a perpetual Verdure; the Walks are made firm enough with a sort of Gravel they get out of the River; the Orangery is counted one of the largest in all Europe; there are beautiful Cascades, and there is a perfect Theatre excellently cut out into green Seats, the dressing-rooms for the Actors being so many Bowers and Summer-houses on each side, the whole set off with many fine Statues, most of 'em gilt, and an excellent Water-work just behind.

9. THE Electoral Prince, GEORGE AUGUSTUS, was born the 30th of October, N.S. 1683. He gives the greatest hopes of himself that we or any People on Earth cou'd desire; and tho you saw him your self, yet I shall again revive your Memory on so grateful a Subject. He has a very winning Countenance, is middlesiz'd like his Father, well-made, and of a manly Aspect and Deportment. He speaks very gracefully, and with the greatest Easiness imaginable. His Complexion is fair, and his Hair of a light brown. He has had very good Foundations of Learning, as well as his Father who speaks Latin fluently; and all due care has bin taken to furnish him with such other Accomplishments, as are fit for a Gentleman and a Prince, nor can any body better perform his Exercises. He's for his Years a great Master of History, and is in this, as in all things else, extraordinary curious and inquisitive, which is the best and surest Foundation of useful Knowlege. These acquir'd Parts, with a generous Disposition and virtuous Inclinations, will deservedly render him the Darling of our People, and probably grace the English Throne with a most knowing Prince. He learns English with inexpressible Facility. Hitherto he has bin kept wholly free from all Vices, and has not only learn'd of his Grandmother to have a real esteem for Englishmen, but he likewise entertains a high Notion of the Wisdom, Goodness, and Power of the English Government, concerning which I heard him to my great Satisfaction ask several pertinent Questions, and such as betoken'd no mean or common Observation. I was surpriz'd to find he

understood so much of our Affairs already, but his great Vivacity will not let him be ignorant of any thing. There's nothing more left to be wish'd, but that he be proof against the Temtations which accompany Greatness, and defended from the poisonous Infection of Flatterers, who are the greatest Bane of Societys, and commonly occasion the Ruin of Princes, if not in their Lives, yet at least in their Fame and Reputation. I must not omit here to put you in mind with what Affection the late King receiv'd the young Prince at Loo, when the Duke of ZELL brought him to wait on his Majesty; and I particularly remember you us'd to observe with Pleasure, that he caress'd him rather with the fondness of a Father, than treated him with the respect that was due to a Prince of his Rank.

10. THE Elector has no other Children but the young Princess SOPHIA DOROTHY, who was born the 16th of March N.S. 1687. You may depend upon it, SIR, that I am not dazl'd by the Splendor of her superior Condition, nor biased by our ordinary Complaisance for the softer Sex, when I assure you that she's one of the most lovely and charming young Ladys I ever saw. She's admirably well shap'd, tall enough for one of her Years, of a sweet and ingaging Aspect. The Color of her Hair is a fine brown, which to a clear Complexion (and such is her's) is a very great Grace and Ornament. But yet nothing can compare with her Eyes of a very lively blue, wherin she excedes all those of this Court. In the rest of her Features (to show that I won't flatter even a

Princess) I have seen other Beautys who might com in competition with her. And yet, as I told you before, she's really very handsom, and the Lineaments of her Face are duly regular. Her Education is sutable to her Quality; and I need say no more of it, when I say that she's govern'd by the Orders, and under the Inspection of her most illustrious Grandmother, whose Example alone is the best Pattern which any Woman can imitat or propose. She's very happy in the Endowments of her Mind, tho perhaps you'l say that it's a matter which dos not much concern us; yet doubtless you'd retract such a Notion, when you consider'd, that if the Prince dy without Children (which God forbid) she's to succede to the Crown of England preferably to her Uncles, and all the rest of her Family. But to do Justice to every body, in minding her Discourse with others, and by what she was pleas'd to say to my self, she appears to have a more than ordinary share of good Sense and Wit. The whole Town and Court commend the easiness of her Manners, and the evenness of her Disposition; but above all her other Qualitys they highly extol her good Humor, which is the most valuable Endowment of either Sex, and the Foundation of most other Virtues. Upon the whole, considering her personal Merit, and the Dignity of her Family, I heartily wish and hope to see her one day Queen of Sweden.

11. THE Elector's next Brother, Prince MAXIMILIAN WILLIAM, was born the 13th of December, N.S. 1666. I never saw him, he being a General Officer

under the Emperor; so is likewise Prince * CHRISTIAN, who was born the 19th of September, N.S. 1671. The youngest of all, Prince ERNEST AUGUSTUS (call'd after his Father) was born the seventh of September, N.S. 1674. He makes the present Campaign under his Grace the Duke of MARLBOROUGH, and is a Prince of a mild Temper, with very commendable Dispositions. There were two Brothers more kill'd in Hungary, whose Ages or Names it dos not import you to know. And now, SIR, I have given you the truest and most exact Account of this Family that was possible for me, but without any Disguise or Partiality, according to my own Inclinations, and in obedience to your Desires I well know the Affection you bear their Highnesses, not out of any personal Regards or Expectations (above which your Fortune has plac'd you) but as to Princes that have always govern'd in their own Country for the good of their People, and that are in time like to be more nearly concerned with your Provinces, as well as in a better Condition to maintain the Protestant Religion, and to defend the Liberty of Europe. From these Considerations I promise my self that you'l be pleas'd with my Relation, and forgive those Imperfections which the little Time you allow'd wou'd not permit me to supply. And upon the whole, if you find that I am less addicted to censure than to praise (contrary to the custom of the malicious and designing World) you are not to think for all this that I pretend to more good Nature than other People, but that I really found less matter

* *Since kill'd in the Danube*

to blame: for as to any minute Circumstances, or the common Imbecillitys of human Nature (from which you are not to imagin the Persons of this Family peculiarly exemted) these are things to be suppos'd in our ordinary Discourses of all Men, but are not worth relating, when they have no Influence on their public Actions, and that they are fully aton'd and eclips'd by their numerous Virtues. Were it true (as you know it to be most false) that I was banish'd from that Court, and from this where I have the Honor now to reside, which som People report in England at this very time; yet in strict Justice I cou'd give no other Account, than what hereby I send you. Let me add that (contrary to the wicked aspersions and fond wishes of the same Tribe) there is no manner of misunderstanding between our most gracious Queen Anne and that Court, where I dare be bold to affirm that more Respect is paid to her Person, and more Justice don to her Merit, than at home in her own Kingdoms: for there 'tis notorious that several question her Title, who also reflect on her Administration; wheras here the Right of the first is readily admitted, and the Wisdom of the last is highly applauded by all without exception, but by none so much as those who are the best able to judg in such Cases, and who so far look on her Majesty as the unchangeable Friend and Benefactress of their House, that they absolutely resign the whole care of their Interest to her management, and never in the least intermeddle (as other design'd Successors have don) in the domestic Affairs, or Partys, or Parlaments of England, tho nothing transacted there escapes their Cognisance or Information. 'Tis impossible for me to express in how high degrees of Respect and Veneration the Memory of King WILLIAM (the Restorer of the English and the Supporter of the European Liberty) is held in the Court of Hanover; but besides the particular Gratitude they ow him in that place, there is likewise such an Admiration paid to his heroic Qualitys (as there was an intire Deference given to his Judgment when alive) all over Germany, that I'll say no more of it, either as a Fact in it self remarkable, or to you unknown. If I have made no mention of certain other things you desir'd, sufficient amends will be made for those Omissions hereafter. In the mean time I am,

SIR,

Your most oblig'd

and most humble Servant,

TOLAND.

APPENDIX.

THE last Action of King WILLIAM's Exercise of his Kingly Power, was giving the Royal Assent to the following *Oath of Abjuration*. His Strength was so far decayed, that he cou'd not hold a Pen in his Hand, and therfore was oblig'd to stamp his Name to the Commission for passing the Act, on Saturday in the Afternoon; for he dy'd the next Morning before nine of the Clock, Sunday March the eighth, 1701/2.[19] Thus he confirmed to Posterity with his expiring Breath that Liberty civil and religious, for which during his Life he so often fought in the Field, which he was indefatigably augmenting and establishing in his Parlaments, which he was continually bringing to perfection in his Counsils, and which, on his Accession to the Throne, he promis'd (as he has faithfully performed) to secure against all future Attemts to subvert it; wherby we now hold indeed in our Disposition (what we frequently pretended before but in Words) the Balance of Peace and War among the Potentats of Christendom.

2. IN all these Particulars our most excellent Queen ANNE has closely pursu'd his Measures, and in som things outgon the Wishes of that immortal Hero, not only in her unparallel'd Successes against the

common Enemys of Europe, by her fortunat, wise, and victorious General, his Grace the Duke of MARLBOROUGH, Prince of the Holy Roman Empire; but especially in her sollicitous Care for preserving the Succession of the Crown in the Protestant Line of the most Serene House of Hanover, by *a Clause* she has pass'd into a Law in the first Session of her present Parlament, which makes it high Treason for any Person to Write or speak against that most seasonable, necessary, and prudent Establishment, and which I have added here together with the *Oath of Abjuration*. Long may her Majesty reign, to be adding incessantly to her Triumphs over faithless and routed Tyrants, to be the glorious Deliverer of oppress'd Princes and States, to be the firm Support of her numerous Dependents and Allys, for the Protection of the Protestant Interest of all Denominations in all places, and for maintaining of impartial Liberty, unbounded Prosperity, and undisturb'd Peace, in her own most florishing Dominions! Amen.

The Oath of Abjuration.

I A.B. *Do truly and sincerely acknowlege, profess, testify, and declare in my Conscience before God and the World, That our Soverein Lady Queen* ANNE *is lawful and rightful Queen of this Realm, and of all other her Majesty Dominions and Countrys therunto belonging.*

AND I do solemnly and sincerely declare, That I do believe in my Conscience that the Person pretended to be Prince of Wales, during the Life of the late King JAMES, *and since his Decease pretending to be, and taking upon him the Stile and Title of King of England, by the Name of* JAMES *the Third, has not any Right or Title whatsoever to the Crown of this Realm, or Any other the Dominions therto belonging: And I do renounce, refuse, and abjure any Allegiance or Obedience to him.*

AND I do swear that I will bear faith and true Allegiance to her Majesty Queen ANNE, *and Her will defend to the utmost of my Power, against all traiterous Conspiracys and Attemts whatsoever, which shall be made against her Person, Crown, or Dignity: and I will do my best Endeavor to disclose and make known to her Majesty and her Successors, all Treason and traiterous Conspiracys which I shall know to be against Her or any of them.*

AND I do faithfully promise, to the utmost of my Power, to support, maintain, and defend the Limitation and Succession of the Crown against him the said JAMES, *and all other Persons whatsoever, as the same is and stands limited* [*by an Act intitul'd,* An Act declaring the Rights and Libertys of the Subject, and settling the Succession of the Crown] *to her present Majesty, and the Heirs of her Body, being Protestants: and as the same* [*by one other Act intitul'd,* An Act for the further Limitation of the Crown, and better securing the Rights and Libertys of the Subject] *is and stands limited after the Decease of her Majesty, and for Default of Issue of her Majesty, to the Princess* SOPHIA, *Electress and Dutchess Dowager of Hanover, and the Heirs of her Body, being Protestants.*

AND all these things I do plainly and sincerely acknowlege and swear, according to these express Words by me spoken, and according to the plain and common Sense and Understanding of the same Words, without any Equivocation, Mental Evasion, or secret Reservation whatsoever: and I do make this Recognition, Acknowlegement, Abjuration, Renunciation, and Promise, heartily, willingly, and truly, upon the true Faith of a Christian.

So help me GOD.

The Clause making it High Treason to oppose by Word or Writing the Succession in the Protestant Line.

AND for the further securing of her Majesty's Person, and, the Succession of the Crown in the Protestant Line, and for extinguishing the Hopes of the pretended Prince of WALES, *and all other Pretenders, and their open and secret Abettors; be it further enacted by the aforesaid Authority, That if any Person or Persons at any time after the first day of March, One Thousand seven Hundred and Two, shall endeavor to deprive or hinder any Person who shall be the next, in Succession to the Crown for the time-being, according to the Limitations in an Act intitul'd,* An Act declaring the Rights and Liberty s of the Subject, and settling the Succession of the Crown, *and according,to one other Act intitul'd,* An Act for the further Limitation of the Crown, and better securing the Rights and Libertys of the Subject, *from succeeding after the Decease of her Majesty (whom GOD long preserve) to the Imperial Crown of this Realm, and the Dominions and Territorys therunto belonging, according to the Limitations of the aforemention'd Acts: That is to say such Issue of her Majesty's Body, as shall from time to time be next in Succession to the Crown, if it shall please God Almighty to bless her Majesty with*

Issue, and during the Time her Majesty shall have no Issue, the Princess SOPHIA *Electress and Dutchess Dowager of* Hanover, *and after the Decease of the said Princess* SOPHIA, *the next in Succession to the Crown for the time being according to the Limitation of the said Acts, and the same maliciously, advisedly, and directly shall attempt by any Overt Act or Deed; every such Offence shall be adjudg'd High Treason, and the Offender or Offenders therin, their Abettors, or Procurers, and Comforters, knowing the said Offence to be don, being therof convicted and attainted according to the Laws and Statutes of this Realm, shall be deemed and adjudged Traitors, and shall suffer the Pains of Death, and all Losses and Forfeitures, as in Cases of High Treason.*

THE END.

Editor's Notes

1. This refers to the Act of Settlement, 1701 which decided the succession to the English throne (see *Foreword*). Toland refers to it as the 'Act of Succession' throughout the text.
2. See *Errata*, page 12, line 3 in original.
3. See *Errata*, page 18, line 5 in original.
4. See *Errata*, page 23, line 28 in original.
5. Sic. A misspelling for Oranienburg.
6. Sic. A misspelling for Potsdam.
7. See Note 5 above.
8. See Note 5 above.
9. See Note 5 above.
10. See Note 4 above.
11. See *Errata*, page 32, line 13 in orginal.
12. See *Errata*, page 35, line 26 in orginal.
13. See Note 4 above.
14. Sic. The numbering sequence suggests that this should be listed as paragraph 20.
15. See *Errata*, page 51, line 17 in orginal.
16. See *Errata*, page 53, line 4 in original.
17. See *Errata*, page 60, line 26 in original.
18. See *Errata*, page 70, line 12 in original.
19. Until 1750, the New Year was deemed to begin on March 25th, the Feast of the Annunciation, in Great Britain (excluding Scotland).

Further Reading

JN Duggan: *John Toland: Ireland's Forgotten Philosopher, Scholar ... and Heretic.* Published by The Manuscript Publisher in print and e-book editions. First published in 2010.

JN Duggan: *Sophia of Hanover: from Winter Princess to Heiress of Great Britain*, Peter Owen Publishers, London 2010.

Ragnhild Hatton: *George I: Elector and King*, Thames and Hudson, London 1978.

Sophie de Hanovre: Mémoires et Lettres de Voyage, ed. **Dirk Van der Cruysse**, Fayard, Paris 1989.

Chronology of Toland, his life and times

1603 James I/VI succeeds to the English throne.

1606 Ulster Plantations begin.

1613 Henri IV of France assassinated, Louis XIII succeeds to French throne.

1625 James I/VI dies, Charles I succeeds to thrones of England and Scotland.

1642 Start of English Civil War.

1645 Louis XIII dies, Louis XIV succeeds to French throne.

1649 Charles I beheaded January 30th.
Cromwell besieges Drogheda and Wexford.

1660 Charles II restored to English throne.

1670 John Toland born November 30th.

1677 William of Orange marries Mary Stuart.

1685 Charles II dies, succeeded by James II.
Revocation of the Edict of Nantes.

1686 John Toland joins Church of Ireland.

1687 Goes to Glasgow University.

1688 William of Orange invades England.

1689 William and Mary crowned King and Queen of England.

1690 Williamite War in Ireland. The Battle of the Boyne marks the turning point though the war itself was not concluded until 1691.

1696 *Christianity not Mysterious* published.

1697 *An Apology for Mr. Toland etc.* published, also *A Defence of Mr Toland in a letter to Himself.*

1698 Toland's *The Life of John Milton* published.

1699 *Amyntor; or a defence of John Milton* published.

1700 *The Life of James Harrington* published.

1701 Act of Settlement (aka Act of Succession) is passed.

Anglia Libera: or The Limitation and Succession of the Crown of England explained and asserted published.

Toland accompanies Lord Macclesfield to Hanover.

1702 William of Orange dies, succeeded by Queen Anne.

War of the Spanish Succession begins.

Toland in Berlin.

1704 *Letters to Serena* published.

Battle of Blenheim.

1705 Sophia Charlotte, Queen of Prussia dies 1st February.

An Account of the Courts of Prussia and Hanover published.

1712 *A Letter against Popery* by Sophia Charlotte of Prussia, (edited by Toland) published.

1714 Sophia of Hanover dies 8th June.

Queen Anne dies August 1st, succeeded by George I.

1715 Louis XIV dies, succeeded by Louis XV, France ruled by the Regent.

1718 *Nazarenus: or Jewish, Gentile, and Mahometan Christianity* published.

1722 Toland dies in London 11th March.

ABOUT THIS BOOK

This book has also been published as a Kindle edition - find it on Amazon

OTHER BOOKS BY JOHN TOLAND

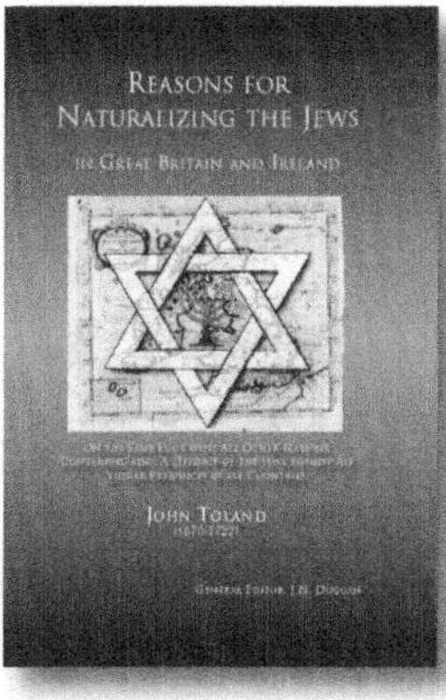

Reasons for Naturalizing the Jews in Great Britain and Ireland (1714)

by John Toland

General Editor: J.N. Duggan

Published by **The Manuscript Publisher** (2013) and available in print and e-book editions. Further information about these and other titles is available from the websites of **The Manuscript Publisher** and **Books by J.N. Duggan**:

www.TheManuscriptPublisher.com/bookshop

and

BooksbyJNDuggan.com

OTHER BOOKS TO READ:

John Toland: Ireland's Forgotten

Philosopher, Scholar …

and Heretic

by J.N. Duggan

Available in print and e-book editions.

For further information please visit the

websites of:

TheManuscriptPublisher.com/bookshop

and BooksbyJNDuggan.com

ALSO BY J.N. DUGGAN

Sophia of Hanover: from Winter

Princess to Heiress of Great Britain,

1630-1714

Published by Peter Owen Publishers,

London, 2010

ISBN: 978 0 7206 1342 1

Available to Buy Online:

www.BooksbyJNDuggan.com

COMING SOON:

Hans Axel Fersen: portrait of a gentleman

by J.N. Duggan

Publication Date: spring 2014

Made in the USA
Monee, IL
08 November 2026

67380518R00059